21 Sirens and How To Drown Them

Claudia Hutchinson

BookLeaf Publishing

Claudia Hutchinson

Presentation by *BookLeaf Publishing*

Web: www.bookleafpub.com

E-mail: info@bookleafpub.com

About Author's Photography by Jill Kerswill

ISBN: 978-93-5744-967-0

First edition 2022

To each Red Riding Hood who swallowed their Wolf or is still mid-digestion and to those whose Sirens drown from the inside. You are a most amazing poetry of teeth and flooding. Unalone and beautiful despite their whispers.

ACKNOWLEDGEMENT

This book is my heart in many ways, but it couldn't have been possible without the support and encouragement of quite a few important people and/or anatomies.

Firstly, my highschool English teacher Mr Simon Kindt, who is an incredible Brisbane poet in his own right as well as a wonderful teacher and person. I will never forget your quirky toe shoes, and of course the way you influenced poetry into my life as a way to express the things I couldn't have otherwise. I'm sure that your intention was- in its origin- not so blatantly grand as it was just to encourage the passion of the spoken and written word in general youth, though in that you consistently succeed. Nonetheless, your introduction to fifteen year-old me who somehow thought all my poetry had to rhyme into slam poetry as an art form was inspiring. No matter what I wrote, or how I wanted to perform my pieces, you were an accumulation of incredible support, advice and encouragement. Your influence since then has enhanced my love of poetry into something grander, which provides for me a foundation of which I can stack, topple, and rebuild myself on.

My thanks is then further extended to my friends Elaine, Matt, Quinn, Riley, and Tully who have, in mixture, supported me throughout my early poetry days to my modern; coming to my performances, reading over my work and in earlier days making me passionately read the labels of shopping products in what they called *"My Slam Poet Voice"* for their own amusement.

I thank them all affectionately for their unrelentless support in both creativity and friendship despite the drowning songs of their own sirens.

This is specifically emphasized in regards to this particular book, where if not for my dear friend Quinn who sent me the BookLeaf writing challenge in the first place, this publication would have never come into reality. In regards to the beautiful illustrations done by Laveen and their team (who was wonderfully patient with me and my vision), I extend a further accreditation to Elaine who provided me much assistance with their witchy prowess and knowledge of tarot cards. Conversing through multiple phone calls, mediums, and phone failures as I partook in Brisbane's trademark public transport, your resilience and detailing for the attribution of major arcana to each of my poems was a more than stellar effort, perfect for one so often associated with the moon. I also once again thank Riley who assisted me in ideas for the illustrations my brain was empty of and got those cogs turning.

To the above friends in addition to my two sets of parents and my unofficial sister Dhanesh who have listened to my performances from couches, the backs of theater's during splits in hours and made an effort to encourage me in this publication, I give my thanks and acknowledgement for going above and beyond to support me in this exciting endeavor.

My last and final thanks in great humor goes to my editors and BookLeaf Publishing who thankfully let me change my preface to what it is today from the accidental submission filler of '*I wrote this book*' it could have been. In this case, I do not credit the friends who told me to keep it because they thought it hilarious.

PREFACE

21 Sirens and How to Drown Them is a collection of poetry written over my 21 Years. To encapsulate this, it is also 21 poems exactly. A sort of underworld katabasis and fairytale, it is my experience of battle cry- at times a snarl, gasp, weep, or a bite.

A circus mirror hall of inner demons, the collection has moments where it is fierce while in others flowery. Going beyond the dragonslaying where perhaps the most powerful pause is where the experience was just pretty and words and I thought of simply writing something beautiful. Those poems represent intermissions where the sirens have temporarily been silenced, where both author and reader are mast-tied Odysseus and his wax eared crew mates immune to their siren's song.

It is no surprise to anyone who knows me well that my poetry is highlighted thickly with my own personal diction. Making it hard to find many poems in the collection that are not touched by my allusions to famous works of English literature, ancient history, mythos as well as stories of Grimm fairy tales and modern horror filmography.

As a matter of fact, there is a deeper elucidation in effect in the form of the illustrations which -following the 21 number theme- highlight the journey of '*The Fool*' in the form of the 21 major arcana cards of a tarot deck. They are at times either reversed or upright to both mirror the poem and create their own commentary on their deeper inner demon representation. Since they are in many ways elaborating on the story of each poem and its significance, it's only fitting that they -in their own symbolic way-represent this journey. As such, 'The Fool' card illustration is the book's cover, representing ends and beginnings with the other cards/poems shedding light on the journey thus far.

Through a complete read-through the reader may note that some themes or motifs repeat throughout the poetry collection itself; that of 'Atlantis', 'Monsters' and 'Girl' etc. At times these extended metaphors function as a sort of secret key symbolism and are welcomed to be taken as whatever creates meaning to the reader guessed, realized or otherwise. It is also due to them that the order the poems are presented in is somewhat important. With some poems referencing back and forward between other pieces in the collection to function as a sort of building poetic crescendo and/or a contextual foreshadowing.

The reader may also note that within the book exists this not so subtle subtext of womanhood and the figure of man that haunts it. For the me who is now a woman in my early twenties, (especially as a bisexual woman, often deplorably fetishised in male culture) this is an important narrative to write in a story about sirens whose voice and songs overwhelms and overpowers them.

The transition from girl to woman which appears another lr undertone in this collection can not be themed without addressing the normalization of harassment in culture and male gaze. As such, this frustration, anxiety, fear, and rage is inspired both in my own experiences and that which I have witnessed in the women around me in their own. These flashes of red feature here as dedications and acknowledgements of these unanimous experiences.

Knowing all of the above milieu, I hope you, the reader, enjoy the experience of this collection.

Whether reading aloud or to yourself, please know that you are never alone in your battles. For me this collection is the show down in which I drown my own sirens, speaking them in and out of existence. Whilst my self-expression lies in poetry, it should be emphasized that everyone has their own way and modus operandi with what's important being what works for you. Sometimes it may succeed in temporary results, occasionally the long term. You learn to accept your Sirens and hum over the sound of them and that's how you finally submerge them. For me at least, it's clear the battle isn't over yet, that it's a battle won in an ongoing inner war. However, by publishing this work and succeeding in my forever dream (despite the inner voice that said it would never come into fruition) I have begun the process. This book is very much a big step to reaching the point where I can outsing any future Siren that sings my way.

TRIGGER WARNING

This collection of poetry explores themes of mental health, creative formating, existential dread, extended metaphors, sexual assault and some badass feminism. Do note that the poetic descriptions aren't particularly grapphic, except for the feminism because it should be.

XI

JUSTICE

A Shopping List For Boys Who Will Be Boys and Girls Who Will Be Monsters

- [x] ~~Do not feature me in your perfume,~~
- [x] ~~But swallow in your arsenic.~~
- [x] ~~Do not hold me to the moon,~~
- [x] ~~But know that I am part of it.~~
- [x] ~~Do not sculpt me Aphrodite,~~
- [x] ~~But shoot me as hunted Artemis.~~
- [ ] Do not see a sweetened girl,
- [ ] See the creature that made art of it.

II
HIGH PRIESTESS

Shipwreck

/Ship-rek/
noun

1. The act of self-destruction when in the water, of wearing gloves to hide the barnacles between your finger bones.

2. You learn how to ballroom dance with your father's ghost. Every step like a tsunami, chaotic fingertip foam and hair salt excretion. He sings like an anchor and weighs you down much the same way, the wavelength and body of every echo.

3. You see your grandmother in the mirror more times than you can count, blue to her lips and rattling on the inside. She distorts her reflection intentionally, likes the idea of ripple and ash and that things that are true aren't always what they should be. She names you Thalassa, and burns your immortality away through blackout chandeliers and empty dinner parties. You erase it from your mind as it erases you, the kind of memory that remembers being forgotten.

4. The sirens are bleeding out a tune on the nearest sea rock and it goes '*It's a secret how you're awake*.' You close your eyes at the sound of it. Peaceful mid-drown, dislocate your pelican wings over the island and bath yourself in sand like it could freeze. Open your cavern mouth, all pearl and clam with the stolen ships inside, set your wings ablaze underwater and dispose of the key.

5. She dallies too much in ghosts that she learned how to become one. Makes her home under an iceberg, as a human Titanic. Goes under water, dances with her Fathers ghost and drowns in her words.

6. '*There's no place like home*.'

XV

THE DEVIL

Daddy Likes His Death Between His Teeth

Daddy likes his death between his teeth,
Likes the way he holds it there,
Between his two middle fingers in the dirt.
Daddy's got clockwork lips,
Got cogs spinning,
                    Time-clicking,
Every time he puts his little-big Death to his mouth.

But Daddy got a life that poured from his broken ribcage,
Daddy got himself a little Half-Mirror,
With big blue eyes!
But that ain't all there is,
To the all of a broken truth in dove flight,
Wings spreading,
                    Feet forgetting,
                                        To lift off.

Half Mirror's got herself a little broken truth,
In the firefly bottles,
She hangs on the angel's hanging tree.
Stores Daddy's secrets in them like blood liquor,

Diffusing in the creek.
She watches them illuminate,
In the string of half bled red moonlight.
Closes her rosemary-blue eyelids to remember,
How Daddy unhinges his jaw every morning,
On the bathroom sink,
With his cut off wedding finger.
Cause Daddy keeps looking
Up,
Up,
Up
But don't see stars,
Doesn't see light,
Sees nothing but fading blotches,
With grey streaks.
Fadin',
Fading,
Oh,
Daddy
is *fading,*
fast.

Half-Mirror knows he wakes up to the sun,
Crying black-widow brides,
And shovels himself a sky-earth.
Remembers how he tells her,
That it helps him see in greys,
Rather than bloods' and skys.

Helps him retrace footprints on hourglass sand.
But Half-Mirror don't understand what's so important,
About kissing <u>lines</u> and *waves* in dirt.
Like mother earth,
Wasn't already a mother to hell as well,
But Daddy hell doesn't come from the earth,
It comes from people.
Don't give into the temptation,
Because it is a mouthy cavern,
That
Is e a t i n g
You a w a y.

But Daddy don't stop reaching out a hand,
Like pulling aces from spades,
Bruisin' sky's eyes till bags lay under;
Dead mango,
Bruised mango.
Mango turned grey in-
Three,
T w o,
O n e,
Wilted **dead thing** in her heart strings.

Daddy's asking to taste fire again,
To spin planets,

On the clicks and waves of his tongue,
With the peel of his gum flesh,
Playing *God*,
Like children play hide and seek,
And old men play cards,
Starting on hearts and diamonds.
And trading for *clubs and spades!*
But Half-Mirrors don't know the balance,
Of men and their treacherous fate.

Girl's a glass waiver,
Braiding shards of glass into her hair,
Instead of flowers.
                                        Half-Mirror's paused. . .
Trapped between t w o
                                                closing in maze /doors,
                                                Daedalus labyrinth.
But Daddy does and should know that hell,
Comes in the form,
Of a little-square-box to this girl.
Knows that Half-Mirror's oversized eyes,
See the devil's smirk from where he stands,
Behind Daddy's matching pair,
{Well they're black now anyway.}

No Half-Mirror's lost her reflection now!
Daddy,

Don't have glass bottle-blue eyes no more, *{He's just got glass.}*

Because Daddy don't see in colour,
Daddy's pulled them out from their flesh roots,
And handed him his eyes.
{Daddy doesn't see-
-Can't see her,}
Just smells the burning rubber smoke,
He wants to run away from,
Not knowing it's in him now,
Not seeing how Lucifer's smirking,
The same way he did,
Before he
f
e
l
l
from *God.*

Half-Mirror's yelling,
Seeing the blood on her hands,
She's a killer now.
Because handing Daddy hell,
Handing him box was the same,
As helping drive that knife into his heart,
The same as watching the life,
Drain from his eyes.

Daddy don't know,
How the devil leaves out of his ears at night,
And leaves drops of his blood,
On her windowsill for Half-Mirror to find,
And wipe away.
{Evidence disposal}

She's standing there watching,
Daddy shove away monsters in the dark.
Daddy's blind now,
Burning accidental suicide,
While she can't do nothin but watch.
Monster's in him now,
Sliding
d
o
w
n
his lungs,
Taking life into his own hands,
And shovin' it down his throat.

Half-Mirror's waiting for the day,
Where midnight wears her thick to her eyes,
And she don't see no more either.
Cause she's knows that when he left,
She left with him,

And now she's a crooked Death-Mirror,
Instead of a half-one.
She's one of them now,
Reflects her Dad again,
In a darker shade of light.
She's what they call a walking graveyard,
And if death could run,
She'd be it mixed with liquor and bad choices,
She no longer feels enough regret too.

So Death-Mirror climbs the sky,
On tears it cried for her daddy,
And now cries for her.
She wraps her finger around the clouds,
And pulls her weight up,
{Scraping off her own fingerprints.}

But there's a guard at the front gate,
And he tells her there's no room for "*her kind*",
That there is on the other side of the blood trail.

But in a blunting-knife truth she's still alive,
And he's still breathing devil smoke,
Still has a chance to hear the smoke alarm,
And turn around.
Still has a chance to know that salvation,
leans in her arms,
Rather than the lit inferno,

From a small little box.
Half-Mirror is still saying to herself,
That there's still time for him to r e a l i z e. . .

Because time's no stranger,
Which mean he ain't on either side,
And Daddy still has a chance,
To catch the relay before the cold.
Daddy turns to her,
Eyes turn blue again,
He holds her with a candle flicker,
How she wishes he'd hold her. . .
xHolding time,
Fixing eyes,
Seeing in colour,
Braiding flowers instead of glass.

Knowing that his greatest madness,
Grew from his wisest sanity,
Daddy likes his death between his teeth.

I
THE MAGICIAN

Dyscalculia (An Answer to Why Six is Afraid of Seven)

The numbers are lost to me,
Blurred beyond the page,
The screen,
The thought,
The treasure map and the reconciliation.

Fixated on the jugular,
They are all manners of throat to me.
Tarzan's Jaguar,
A bodily factorial,
Forever awaiting the pounce.

The algebraic skeleton then,
Remains a drunk upon his grandfather clock,
Sculling wine to an ever arithme-ticking tune.
Storing measuring cups,
Through his bony jaw,
He is a carbonizing red bull,
Chasing every remaining unicorn,
To its unfitting sea.

So eight became swallowed by seven,
As even Homer wrote,

History is without its number line,
Now stuffed in Archimedes' throat.
Six has fallen to its drought,
And to the conflict and defeat.
The nine which has been eaten,
Seven's unsuspecting feat.

Eight was infinite with nine one off,
And six who forgot they once were nine,
Once the same but now valued less then,
Mathematically redefined.
A letter would perhaps be better,
Though mighty Pythagoras, Euclid and Thales
Would disagree,
Atlantis drowned in numbers,
To Zeus's thundering decree.

I am the six which watched as nine was
Swallowed,
Then eight and all the rest.
Who saw seven's entourage charade,
Who forced a laugh in their bereft.
Why is six afraid of seven?
I think I now know the answer why;

Once forced to work at my own subtraction,
This Six has chosen not to die.

XIII
DEATH

The Girl Who Fell In Love With Time

(I)

He buries her in the ground,
Gasping through her rose water lips,
A tangle of thorns and veins,
Lit up from the inside like stained church glass.
Planting wildflowers and sprinkling sunflower
seeds on her like hand grenades and fairy dust lit
by starlight,
Magic by the right of science and the divine.
She waits,
and waits,
for him,
Courting hours and days in northern lights,
By the kisses on her neck and collarbone,
By the rate in which roots t a n g l e,
And braid through her hair in forest moss,
Each time he sends the rain d
o
w
n
to her,
Knowing she's never known anything but the
way,

Water has the tendency to soak through.

(II)

Flooding her through her skin,
Rainbow through her cheekbones,
Ocean floating in a glass bottle.
He sends the water d
o
w
n
Tied in festival ribbons and velvet bows.
And she let's the water d r o p l e t s ,
Ink themself to her skin,
Like cold breaths on summer evenings,
And catches them on her tongue,
Like f
a
l
l
i
n
g

stars,

Letting them d
r
o
p
down like paint,
H o v e r like snowflakes in the air before
dyeing the water inside her.
When he comes,
She warms her palms with her lips and sighs out
skies for him;
Sunsets,
eclipses,
twilights
and *shooting stars*,
And tries to kiss them onto his skin,
Like curled ink love letters from
beneath

The ground.

(III)

It's at times like this when he no longer rains on
her,
That she feels herself e v a p o r a t e ,
Shatters her love for him backwards onto
herself,

A mirror under

~~~~~

the sea.
A series of vibrations crawling along her bones,
Lost cities rising above

~~~~~~~~~~~~~~~~~

the ocean water,
Her love for him rebounding onto her skin like gold paintings,
Moving with the phases of the moon.
Because when he parts with her skies,
Her lips part clouds,
And remove moons
From their places in out-of-space
And manifest within her chest:

o
o n
M s
orbiting
m s
o n
o

And when he comes back he lies above her,
Touching her through soil,
And light flickers of candles,

Hoping that she'll feel the heatand use it as a
substitute for his own.

(IV)

She falls asleep

____

under him then,
Eyelids feathered.
Whispers to him from b
e
l
o
w
the ground.
though she does not have the ability to speak.
Fertilizes the ground above her,

____

Below him,
Into flowers and bluebirds,
Flying
u
p
to him.
So when he wakes he knows she felt him there,
And knew him then in a fractioned-

<u>moment of time,</u>

Passing in the speed of light to the clash of,
Planets as they crash into each other,
As sunsets and evenings fight each other for the sky's affection.
For a lover.
Spreading out – in –
Above
And under.

As above–

―――――――

So below.

(V)

She lives for his mumbled words as he reads to her,
Understanding only the c l i c k s,
Of cogs in his cheeks,
The machine and the pocket watch.
Lulled to sleep,
By the vibrations of his steps on the ground,

a
b
o
v
e
her.
Because truly she is just a girl.
Longing for the day where she knows the things
he breathes and can see them through his eyes,
Where she becomes familiar with *his voice,*
And palms,
And words,
And colour.
She doesn't have a name but she found an
identity in her love for him;

"The Girl Who Fell In Love With Time'

A man who passes her frequently,
Close enough to touch without t o u c h i n g,
To breathe each other's air without each other.
To read without being heard.
Because she burns,
Burns,
Burns,
And he lit her to ice.

To silence,

To whisper...

(VI)

He buries her in the ground,
Gasping through her rose water lips,
A tangle of thorns and veins lit up from the inside like stained church glass.
Planting wildflowers and sprinkling sunflower seeds on her like hand grenades and fairy dust lit by starlight,
Magic by the right of science and the divine.
Growing towards each other,
They don't need words or touch,
But one day he lies looking at the sky thinking of the girl
who lies under him.
Leaves his hand open,
Shuts his eyes,
Listening to the c l i c k of cogs in his cheeks,

The hour he knows is passing.

And one day surrounded with sprinkles,
Of half grown sunflower seeds,
And bluebird's eggs.

She grows out her hand,

Wrapping it closed with his.

And knows not what she is,
But what she could be . .

XVII
THE STAR

Satellite Insomnia

Satellite eyelids and linen skin,
This roof my sheltering orbit.
I fail to see how the dusk,
Turned evening,
Sank to day.

Through the fatal slither of the blind,
The creak in my window,
I see it all.
Sunlight orange on the eyes,
A warming peach on the skin,
But heart forever on the moon.

The twilight then,
Is an ever-twinkling pair of lips,
Curved only to press with night.
A gentle friction of the witching hour.

My mother then,
A dawn-star,
Whispers beyond of only black,
A tale of how it comes,
From the craters in my bloodstream.

How I came out of the womb a set of stars,
With a chest that would hollow out,
For my father-similar solar system.
A darkening fruity cavity,
Medieval and yet Bram Stroker -drawn.

Left for empty of sunlight,
For the spinning of planets instead.
As a self-abandoned astronaut wondering why I
*Ev*er fell in love with space,
'*I am*' I reply,
'*All but twenty one dark sides of the moon.*'

Night-ringer they call me.
To cry upon the spheres,
To spin around the astro-dust,
And tiptoe upon the shadows.
I cough it up like oxygen between my bedsheets.
Something I *never* needed to breathe.

Curled around big toe- to pinkie finger.
I live my days all twelve phases of the moon,
A faded glow of a once familiar sun,
And it's far too rapid solar flare.

I exhale foggily,
A dusking firefly,
Stuck stickily to the muddy creek bed,

Tethered down by bedsheets,
I tear up at the twelve.
The two o'clock,
The three,
Knowing I never wanted to be midnight.

Trapped in the forever feeling memories,
Of a sunflower caught in a moonbeam,
Fades of yellow,
Almost content with withering.

But the fact remains,
That I am one of two hundred,
Solar system moons,
Of perhaps more beyond this Milky Way,
That I am bigger than Pluto.
An astronaut that has floated,
Every light wave of space.
And perhaps with time will realize,
Even I can overshadow a solar eclipse.

VI

THE LOVERS

Love and Reapers

Oh for woe,
That reaper who speaketh of love,
All puckered lips and sharpened scythe,
For you I hand each entanglement of hearty
anatomy.
A predestinate threat of fate,
I am a dripping of a flower's dew upon your
Silky spider's web.
And so I find,
That devastation speaks better in sonnets than in
cheerily rhyme.
Yet make no mistake of the diamond mined
from a collapsing cave,
For I do not mourn the death of bees,
That sting as sharp as their honey sweetens,
As I do kiss each puckered lipped reaper,
In the search for the one that kisses,
But not beckons. . .

VIII
STRENGTH

Final Girl

He's killing in slow motion,
A jump scare film black noir.
He's every screeching violin,
She's babysitting for next door.

Serrating his own ego,
He whispers beyond the phone.
She shivers at the sounds,
His voice Sleepy Hollow acetone

She dies if she has sex,
She bleeds if she's alone.
Brave,
        Beautiful,
                A virgin,
The audience watches her atone.

A wolf in his sheep clothing,
A final girl to the very end,
She grabs the kitchen knives and blades,
To rip black holes within him then.

She has suffered through your prequel,
Then your sequel,
                To the credits.

Let her be the final stab wound,
The audience is famished.

Foaming at the mouth,
The thriller-killer faces down.
But the blonde wins in this one,
And she wins all hands thrown down.

~ *She will not be in your story.*
not anymore . . .

IV

THE EMPEROR

Mouth

My walls have my parents' teeth
White and yellow,
Incisors,
        Plark,
                Fillings and all.
I am chomped from the womb to consume,
Girl-blue-riding hood squashed into the walls of her parent wolf.

You'll find me there gum buried,
Gothic writer naked on the tombstone.
Flesh pressed against their wolf stomach lining like a 1987 pin screen,
Freddie Krueger forming from your bedroom ceiling,
Stomach acid singed.
Joker's favorite hazardous shade of green.
Oh and how you'll hear the stomach rumble to the growl of how this one-
This one-
          Tastes just right.

My house is a mouth,
Is a mouth-

Is a mouth-
Is a mouth-
Is.
A.
Mouth.

I keep whispering to the rats in the roof,
About how my house is a mouth,
And how swimming in its saliva,
warrants the jaws theme.
How the solitude of my hand in the wolf then,
Is a haunting fleshy imprint,
                    Fresh for Halloween.
I explain to its confusion,
                    Its inability to comprehend,
That my family tree runs on the gum-lines,
That I lost too many shoes and then wishes too.
How my dentist architect built it well,
Built it Alice in her Wonderland.
Too Cheshire Cat,
It kept grinning *more-*
                    And more **teeth.**

They told me the blueprints for home,
Didn't specify what kind of mouth.
That the tooth-fairy collected,
Could grow into paining wisdoms,
And so I assumed shark was the brand,

That all mouths came in.
That saliva was meant to be sticky,
Enzyme's always ready for the
b r e a k d o w n,
To keep you tangled beneath tongues,
Long enough to be swallowed down.

My house is a mouth –
Is a mouth–
Is a mouth –
That now has its cavities.
Because what I associated with sugar,
To bleach them a brighter white,
Has stained,
And I have become *sick* of being swallowed.
Of broken teeth-
And rotting gums,
Cigarette lips,
And charcoal tongues,
And being stuck in the in-between of throats and their rising bile,
Because houses were not constructed,
To keep you consumed.

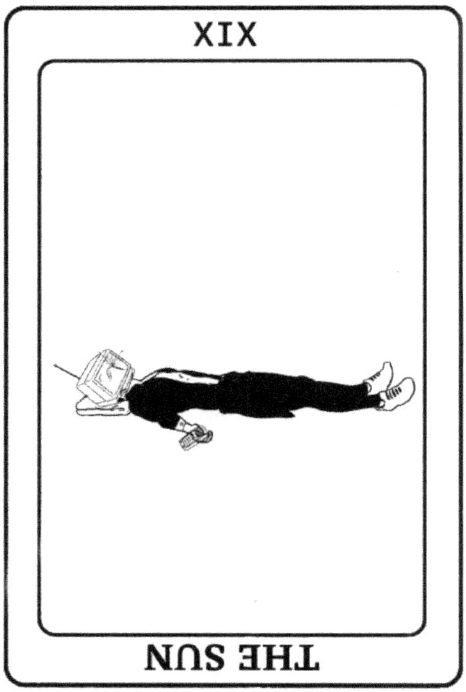
XIX
THE SUN

Static Head (I) - A Prequel

His head's in the static,
[Packing ghosts in the attic
Tongue-tied monochromatic.
And as he desecrates my say,
I wonder if living life,
Means we keep going on this way.
But his head's in the static,
Smiles mannequin plastic,
Snapping thin like elastic.
Tragic and erratic,
His head's in the static,]
And mines,
Trying to keep the static,
Out of me.

XII

THE HANGED MAN

Static Head (II) An Epilogue

Dear Mr Static Man,
You've smashed your head,
Through the television again.
[Grainy on the mind,
Boosting up the dial.
You're a repeating set,
Of cinematic screams.
On the radio,
And I have become sick *of vintage.*
TV forever stuck on the head,
Your breath and eyes in black and white,
Your finger glued to the pause of the remote.
Channel glitching,
Screen Head tilting,
You say TV's got a plan for you.
But the truth is-]
Your Static Daughter
[Gave in to what you taught her]
She shoved her head in the TV
Chasing after you,
And now in all distorted color bars,
She's in the static too.

XIV
TEMPERANCE

Phantom of Intrusive

Attention to the Opera!
And to Phantom's stolen muse,
The noose has taken Paris,
And blade whispers for taboo.

The masquerade has themed me,
Drawn to shatter chandelier.
The intrusive operatic,
To my dies irae ears.

Box five is empty yet again,
The organ a chilling tune.
Raoul has dived from the upper stage,
Into his theatric shade of blue.

I have lit my watered candles,
Like the phases of the moon,
To set the house inferno,
And burn down my wordy fumes.

These thoughts have stolen up the lines,
Their own double-sided mirror,
Seeing out and seeing in
More momentary fire.

'Past the point of no return',
They sing and I refuse,
Unable to shutout,
What they pick and I don't choose.

IX
THE HERMIT

Snow Fall

I wished my lover the hourglass
Time's crown and the raven's hand.
For her I've traded dust,
And alchemized it into sand.

I have grown too tired of time,
But must give something equal in exchange.
While this graveyard has lied to me,
It is the tomb I'll disarrange.

Cog of heart and gear of soul,
We've been clicked back into place.
Separating like oil and heat,
Met with Flamel's slippery embrace.

I had hoped we'd turn to steam I say,
An engine fueled by its own smoke.
Un-Elizabethan and instead Ripper,
We are the revolution revoked.

My lady of the underground,
You have worked the stage of death.
The soil of it yields to you,
And has replaced your heart with breath.

By the winter flakes upon your lashes,
The ablated waste that's shown.
By snowflake and earthquake,
Your tears dry to the bone.

Lover I will wait for you,
So dance upon your extra hour.
From beyond the snowfall wall,
I hold out my icy flower.

When your anger boils you,
And blooms the lilied rose.
I hope you will remember me,
And one day follow where I go.

XVI
THE TOWER

She Left Like

School prepares us for a lot of things,
Molding,
            Forming,
                        "Conforming",
Like one flew o v e r
                        the cuckoo's nest,
Next day didn't fly high enough,
Good enough.
Broken birds' wings painted golden under my eyes,
Mental institutions made of twigs with little "well-made" eggs inside.
School prepares us for a lot of things. . .

But what it doesn't teach you,
Is how to stop sleepwalking,
In the middle of the road in daylight.
How your undergarment tears you,
In your half-asleep reprise in the bathroom mirror,
Your own underblanket mud feet and Victor Pascow,
Your Pennywise blood floating skyward like a red balloon,
                        <u>It has become habit for you,</u>

To sow your own mouth s h u t,
A haunted process,
It has become habit for you.
To rip the threads out with your Arachne fingernails,
Before tugging them back up again.
Pretty-little-pretty-speaking-mechanical thing,
Cogs out the side of the mouth like rotting cigarette butts,
Smoking ten backwards with copper wire hanging out the side of your old western lip.
Cuckoo birds pushing each other out of your ears.
Because what they don't teach you is how to tie a copper corset to your mouth,
And how it feels when you tie it so *tight* that you can't hear yourself breathe.
And what they don't prepare you for is how to fix yourself when the cogs fall out,
And you realize that you were never sleepwalking at all. . .

Because *sir*,
It goes like this,
Goes like *only* this. . .
She left like hurricane,
Cyclone pulling your gums back from your teeth,

Prison cell under the dental chair.
<u>She left like tsunami,</u>
Earthquake,
Shook you out of your surprise,
-Shook me out of my organs-
-My baby eyes,
Shook him back into his,
Crescent nails leaving skin.

He's trapped inside a little reprise of,
'Daddy likes his death between his teeth'
but now he just likes it
E V E R Y W H E R E!

Had alcohol like acid burning his blood,
His perception of her kiss,
A fingerprint on his brain.
No,
She can't kiss you together again,
She kissed you monochrome-
Car without the headlights on-
She kissed you city at midnight-
Black lipstick-
Grim reaper on the upper lip.

She kissed all the seams from your baby eyes,
But *you* kissed you apart.

XX
JUDGEMENT

Fair Lucretia of Sabine

Fair lady of Sabine,
You're behind each set of stairs,
The Alley,
The Bedroom,
The Bar…
Your one dilated eye watchful,
From the erosion of the crack,
He has sculpted you protestingly from concrete,
A cold parody of your fated marble,
You are Perseus slain Medusa
And Poseidon has made white lilies of you.

Flesh against the ionic column,
Your maiden hair in snakes,
They will reminisce on her architecture.
Her underworld foundation,
Feeling suddenly redesigned,
And now anemic with the name he had stolen
from you-
You are all 13's of Winchester house.

Reddening Lady of Sabine,
Lucretia of Conquering Rome,
They will find traces of you,

On his strangers bottom lip,
The arsenic percentage of his cologne.
You are a forever stretching cut upon his heart,
A blooming belladonna,
And each flick of a razor blade upon his throat.

Your watching eye weighing him down,
In each less powerful stride of his,
You metamorphize,
Your own Venus Di Milo,
Fire survived Athena Parthenos,
With your ivory hand-held Nike,
Stronger than any trident,
A High Chariot Boudica never lonesome,
With her battling warrior daughters.

You are a masterpiece of Rome,
And Greece will draw constellations of you.

III
THE EMPRESS

Bathtubs and Helium

ACT 1, Scene 1

With a tilt of wrist from **THE WOMAN'S** *hand upon the tap, The filling will commence. A rising crescendo of water, Sloshed by its motion conductor to the bath rim. In time to this unnerving Beethoven fifth symphony, The dramatis personae of the figure of –*

GIRL IN THE BATHTUB : is introduced. Her pond eyes overflowing, Her body a melting labyrinth of lily pads, skin and water lilies. She exists a set of eyes atop the water, A soaked blooming of purple. Her nymphaeaceae hair a defiance of gravity.

(It is clear from when the scene is set,
That she does not belong here.)

THE FIGURE OF WOMAN HOWEVER: is a victorian silhouette portrait, Who's shadow stretches from the hallway to obscure the natural lighting of the tub. Instead she is red strobe LED. Slasher music.

Her folded Paper boats, placed carefully, will obscure **THE GIRLS'** *lamb figure, And then they will sink.*

ACT 1, Scene 2

THE WOMAN: *(will exit stage left,)* Mona Lisa on the lips, *(And emerges with the helium tank ,Which is all but a kind of shark film scuba gear.)* She will take her nails to the mirror, Till her flesh drips onto the now shattered pieces on the floor.

*(**THE WOMAN** takes a seat then, Tailbone pressed to its cooling texture, Below her an aquarium display of nessy and megalodon.)*

THE FIGURE OF GIRL: is all too focused on their teeth, Pond eyes still watching. Fingers too submerged to move.

THE WOMAN : takes no notice as she drinks the tanks and begins to blow: A human metronome of air and filling.

*(She takes the pieces of **GIRL'S** reflection, Each shard sharper than before, And places them, In each vermillion balloon.)*

ACT 1. Scene 3.

The Bathroom now an indefinite boiler room, It is unclear if the woman bears the intention, Still one-by-one the balloons plop into the bathtub,Till it begins to overflow.

THE WOMAN: slides forth the game: Together they play Battleship, Titanic, Cluedo. It becomes the headline,

*'**THE FIGURE OF WOMAN** did it in the bathtub with the glass balloons.'*

(Little Pennywise clown popping bloody
Helium shouting Hitler like:
"They all float down here."')

THE WOMAN: *(sinks the boats and pops each balloon,)* Winking.

THE GIRL: is already too used to flinching.
***(THE WOMAN** exists the room,)*

LEAVING GIRL: She is still floating,
Lily-pads now an anchor, Heavy on her head,
Watching,

(A dripping to a draining,Her eyes submerge.)

ACT ENDS

X

THE WHEEL OF FORTUNE

Schrödinger's Human

The poets have slept within their census,
Protested to Dylan's words,
"*Do not go gentle into that good night*",
Read on,
          Comma,
                    Mark from what's inferred.

With Emily's fly however,
Buzzing upon my muted ear,
And pearl tags gleaming,
                              Between morgue toes,
I am every bit existential Frankenstein's,
Bloodied *cursive Xs and Os*.

With the Reapers features one,
With no agreeable symmetry to mine,
I use my mid-shiver,
                         River weed,
                              Papyrus fingers,

To ink back my scorned reply;

"On that we are agreed," I seethe,
"But even Victor dreaded sky."

My heart not in the colored glass,
I will not swear upon the horseman,
That Yeats in his Ben Bulben received.
Instead I cast my dreary eye's,
Into the irish freezer cold and undefeated,
To the dream where pale skeleton,
Spied me and then retreated.

Only divine in the dichotomy,
In this frontal lobe's decline,
It is not the dying of light that scares me,
But the dust,
On every Shakespearian
Sleeve of mine.

A Freshly risen vision of le'mort.
A mid-sketching portrait of Jane Doe,
Eyes fixated and dilated on the altar,
Of Parisian catacombs.
It is the ephemeral anonymity that awaits,
That keeps me counting bones.

It's true I fear the Egyptian lotus,
Till it blooms in me at night,
Weeds breaking through the ribcage,
The ankh mid-throat burrowing ,
        Swallow choking,
        On the insect of the scarab,
Which grows into an inevitable mental plight.

It is my wish,
I could just be rage,
Or perhaps accept hate,
In poet Frost's good ice.
        But this flesh that becomes me,
        Makes me nauseous at the sight.

Perhaps it is this mortality,
That becomes me,
When I breathe.
And the cup of it,
        I must swirl to sip,
        Before I'm ready to leave.

Or perhaps there sits the concept,
Of simply dying wrong,
        Of ending unhappy,
        Unaccomplished,
        Mute to my own swansong.

Or if antithetical
Is it not the case,
That living is a scream,
And every loss of grace.
That living's enjoying every improved line,
Of your vintage theater's screening time.

So Dylan Thomas rant to me,
To rage in undying light,
The inevitable question,
Setting minds like ours alight.

I am SchrÖdinger's human,
Squished in predetermined box,
That perhaps,
When opened up,
Will accept life at its cost.

VII
THE CHARIOT

Mannequin and Raven

I may go down in history
As the villain,
All snide remarks.
I heard they played the jaws theme,
As I stepped out of the dark.
But in each empty looming shadow,
I'll be sure to creature feature there.

I sent Freddie Kruger to your room,
To remind you that I care . . .

So yes,
I caught the moth man,
And the mummy,
And the wolf.
I Maryshelled them together,
So you can know just what you took.
And now my heart's a beast,

That is snarling out the steam,
From the fire that is rising,
Out of your voodoo seams.

The raven came a knocking,
So I made sure I wasn't home.
The house creaked and echoed,
So even it wasn't alone.

Though I'm sure the skeletons,
In my closet will keep it company.
Since from my first handed experience,
It's what they've always done for me.

I can't call in a model,
That will help fix your design.
So I hope this mannequin will do,
She smiles far too wide.

But if that's not enough for you,
I'm sure a doll will do,
Sew on some eyes,
And pierce her heart,
And she'll give her soul to you. . .

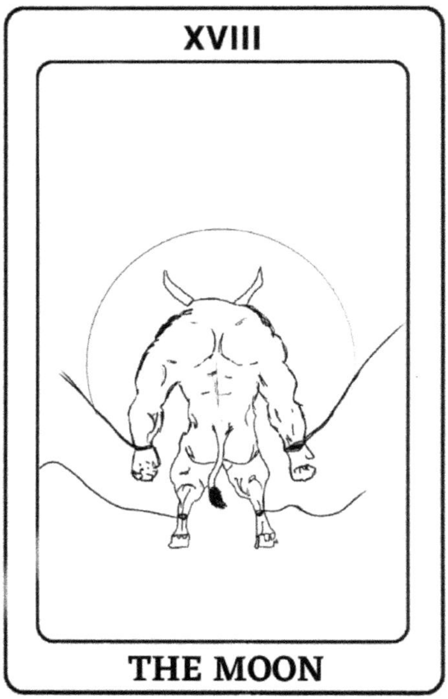
XVIII
THE MOON

Little Brave and Bold

I've burnt down my wonderland,
Too many times to count,
And I've had the sirens teach me,
The many ways to drown
And yet,
        I find in my mind,
                Where I can't sleep at night,
                That I'm alive -
        I'm alive -
I'm alive.

So bring in the soldiers,
Cast them as saints,
                And teach them the war,
                And make me the stakes.
When I shrill each siren,
And the bodies are fakes,
                Then you will remember,
                I have what it takes. . .

I followed after Dante,
But he drew the line.
                He said the mazes,

In these nine circles,
Will drain out what's,
Divine.

But there's a thread that unravels,
And I've come to find,
That the minotaur,
I was so afraid of,
Was this reflection of mine.

So capture the prisoners,
Unmask them as demons,
Punish them with sugar,
And love them with reason.
When I outsing sirens,
And my body's the fake.
Then you will remember,
I have what it takes. . .

I'm little brave and bold,
My heart is but fool's gold.
I'm little though I'm fierce,
I'll preserve what's disappears,
I'm little brave and bold,
My self-vengeance is two fold.

XXI
THE WORLD

I was Atlantis Once

I was Atlantis once,
And they all told me so,
Laurels in the moment,
Above the water,
Gleaming gold.

Now a weakening of aquamarine,
Poseidon-stolen,
Under sea.
He has taken too many notes,
Of Hades and Persephone.

Robbed of Athena's olive tree,
For coral and the weed.
I am Achilles' un-Styx ankles',
Masochistic,
Joke of me.

An Island of Atlas,
Dropped by Titan from the world.
The Anchor weighed,
And Sand dollar,
Nike has left me for the pearl.

Anatomy now waterlogged,
Wax wing melting flesh to spine,
Perhaps over the prophetic fumes,
Did Prythia of Delphi suspect,
That Icarus was mine.

Far behind Hercules' pillar,
One day I fear in history,
They will say I never existed,
But I cannot tell if that scares me more,
Then how Plato still insisted.
But remember till the end,
Of my ruins in the sea.

I was Atlantis once,
And now Atlantis is me.

V
THE HIEROPHANT

I Spoke to God Today

I spoke to God today.
monumental Angel,
sculpting his eyes,
shards of church glass
papermached for skin
to look real,
when the sun shines
through,
A rainbow man in moonlight,
and he spoke of how he could see
right through me
twist my body like clay
through a kaleidoscope,
till it distorted me in the glass,
in his hands.
I spoke to God today. . .
and I realized,
I don't much like
being looked through.
I want to talk God,
there's a few things,
we need to talk about.
like how I carved your figure,

from my cradle
with my broken baby hands,
and watched you decorate,
your Christmas tree,
with your own vocal chords,
to dry out.
to watch them bleed
through the branches.
because every human being when born,
consists of 270 bones,
and he told me
how he liked.
to split them open,
like the branches,
of his bleeding Christmas
tree.
how his greatest talent,
was his ability,
to pluck the feathers,
out of a human skeleton alive,
and do it without looking,
at their faces.
he held his birthday party,
in a graveyard,
blowing up balloons,
on a mass grave,
and told me how he created us,
by carving our minds

out of chipped Angel's tomb stones,
callused fingers,
shaking,
trembling,
chipping us away,
through his mistakes,
like we're all just,
God's figurines,
waxed out of baby sister's hands,
to burn!
ash in the veins,
small church's running away,
with demons locked on the inside.
I'm sorry God.
I know you speak in paradox,
but I speak in statistics,
through your crude humor:
one out of four women,
and six men,
will be sexually assaulted in
their lifetime.
sink it in like acid,
like molten rock and bone,
(like the back feathers-
- *being pulled out)*
and there is an ad,
published red and blue,
found on the back,

of the women's bathroom stall
'*It is the friend*' It says,
'*that you leave behind-*
- that it is the most likely to be raped.'
a rape culture where '*No's*'
taken as '*Yes.*'
and "*if she didn't want to get raped-*
-then she shouldn't have left the house
like that."
Bullcrap!
statistic after statistic
(another chip in an Angel's
tombstone.)
more teenagers and young adults die
from *suicide*,
than from cancer,
AIDS,
heart disease,
stroke,
birth defects,
pneumonia,
influenza,
and chronic lung disease,
combined.
and yet there is something,
ticking away inside of us,
in every passing hour.
a little Tish Thawers going;

"we are the granddaughters-
-of the witches you could never burn!"
The descendants-
of the kings,
you could never defeat.
and we were born,
to be more ablaze then fire,
because darling,

WE.
ARE.
DRAGONS.

and we were sculpted to rage.
rage,
Rage,
RAGE
against the dying of moonlight,
of our own failed humanity!
to paradox,
to spiral,
optical illusion,
out of our own self destruction,
our own blood stream,
and skeleton.
because I spoke to God today,
and watched as he took safety scissors,

to his own halo,
and shredded himself apart,
in front of me.
because the funny thing,
about talking To God,
is that you don't expect him,
to choke on his own name.
we were born to do more than this,
we can be so much more than this,
because demons,
are just the angels,
that refused to stay silent God.
and we know better than anything else
that to slay a monster,
you need to become a bigger one.
a louder one.
because Father,
I spoke to God today,
Mother,
I spoke to God today!
Brothers,
Sisters,
Liars,
Misters,
Catholics,
Atheists,
"Cheese-Panicked Hipsters"
I'm talking to those,

the pinnacle of clinical,
the typical paradisiacal,
waking up,
on a Monday morning,
and working towards a better day.
to the thinkable unsinkables,
and the biblical mythicals,
the reasonable miserables,
and intuitive assuasives,
the warring soarers,
and the imaginative explorers,
the calculative ignorers,
and the dream-scape storers.
and I say:

I spoke to God Today and he didn't hear a word

www.ingramcontent.com/pod-product-compliance
Lightning Source LLC
Chambersburg PA
CBHW051733130826
49812CB00033B/839
9789357449670